The ORTHOPEDIST

by
Lee Jacobs

Photographs by
Gale Zucker

BLACKBIRCH PRESS, INC.

WOODBRIDGE, CONNECTICUT

j616.7
JAC

Published by Blackbirch Press, Inc.
260 Amity Road
Woodbridge, CT 06525

©1999 by Blackbirch Press, Inc.
First Edition

e-mail: staff@blackbirch.com
Web site: www.blackbirch.com

Printed in the United States

10 9 8 7 6 5 4 3 2 1

Acknowledgments
The publisher would like to thank Fletcher Allen Health Care for their valuable cooperation in putting this project together.

Page 12: Artwork by Sonja Kalter

Library of Congress Cataloging-in-Publication Data
Jacobs, Lee.
The orthopedist / by Lee Jacobs : photographs by Gale Zucker.
    p.   cm. — (Doctors in action.)
    Includes index.
    Summary: Uses the daily activities of one doctor to describe the work of an orthopedist.
    ISBN 1-56711-236-6 (lib. bdg. : alk. paper)
    1. Orthopedics—Juvenile literature. 2. Orthopedists—Juvenile literature.
[1. Orthopedics. 2. Orthopedists. 3. Occupations.] I. Zucker, Gale, ill. II. Title. III. Series.
RD732.J33   1999
616.7—dc21
                                     98-3901
                                     CIP
                                     AC

Have you ever broken your arm or leg and had to go to the hospital? If you have, you probably saw an orthopedist. An orthopedist is a doctor who specializes in bones. The term *orthopedic* is from the Greek language. It means "straight child." One of the main things an orthopedist does is make sure your bones stay healthy, strong, and straight!

Orthopedists see patients of all ages. They see newborn babies, elderly people, and everyone in between.

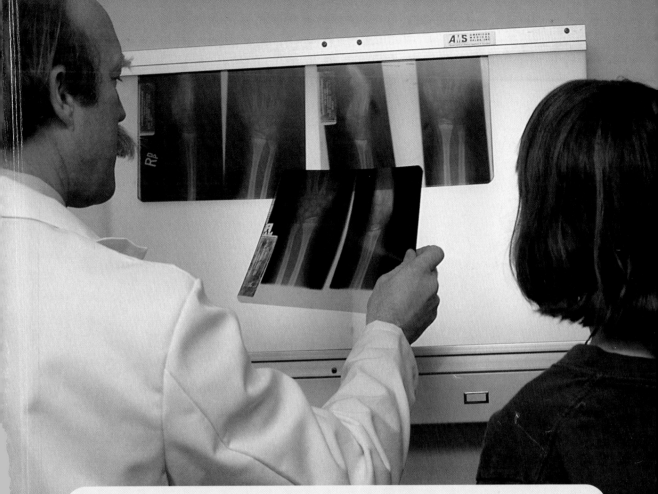

X-ray photographs are one of the best ways for an orthopedist to see the bones inside a body.

Most orthopedists spend a lot of time treating children. Kids may need an orthopedist for many reasons, not just a broken arm or leg. A child may have a sports injury, such as a sprain or break. Or a child may have a long-term problem, such as constant elbow pain from too much Little League pitching! Some kids are born with bone and muscle problems. These children may need the long-term help of an orthopedist.

Dr. Douglas Campbell has been an orthopedist for 17 years. He likes orthopedics because, he says, "I get to treat all kinds of people—young, old, healthy, and sick—and most problems can be fixed in a short time."

YOUR SKELETAL SYSTEM

The bones in your body make up your skeleton. Your skeleton supports your body. It also protects what's inside. Your skull, for example, protects your brain.

An animal that has a spinal column, or backbone, is called a *vertebrate*. Human beings are vertebrates. Your backbone is a row of bones that runs down your back. Your backbone supports the rest of your skeleton. It also protects your spinal cord. Your rib cage protects your heart and lungs.

Each bone in your body is connected to another bone. An adult has 206 bones. Did you know that you have many more bones than your parents? As you get older, some bones in your body grow together, or *fuse*. What is now two or three bones will fuse to become one large bone when you are older!

Bones are held in place by muscle-like things called *ligaments* and *tendons*. These are bands of tough but flexible tissues. These bands allow your skeleton to be flexible. But what makes these hard bones and tough bands able to move? A layer of tissue called muscle.

Your muscles also allow your bones to stay in place when you are not moving! Together, your bones and muscles make up your skeletal system.

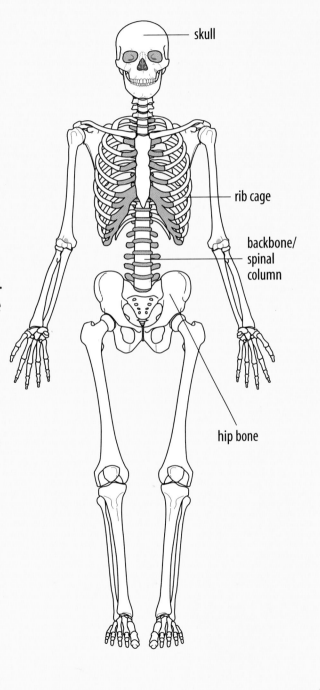

skull

rib cage

backbone/
spinal
column

hip bone

Dr. Campbell's days are very busy! He starts out by "rounding," or visiting patients, at the local hospital.

At the hospital, Dr. Campbell may operate on a patient who needs surgery to fix a problem. This is usually to fix long-term problems that may have been caused by sports injuries or from using joints and ligaments the wrong way.

Another reason Dr. Campbell would make a hospital visit is to see a patient who has recently had surgery. These are called "post-op" (post-operative) patients. He visits these patients mainly to see if they have any questions and to make sure they are healing properly.

Dr. Campbell checks on the progress of a patient who recently had surgery.

At any time of the day or night, Dr. Campbell may be called to the Emergency Room (E.R.). This happens when someone with a broken bone or other similar problem is brought in by ambulance. E.R.s in most hospitals are fast-paced, exciting places!

If you were brought to an E.R. for a broken bone, you might also be seen by a radiologist. That's a doctor who would look at an X-ray to make sure the bone was actually broken. A radiologist is a doctor who specializes in the use of X-rays to recognize and solve medical problems.

Dr. Campbell gets ready for surgery in the Emergency Room.

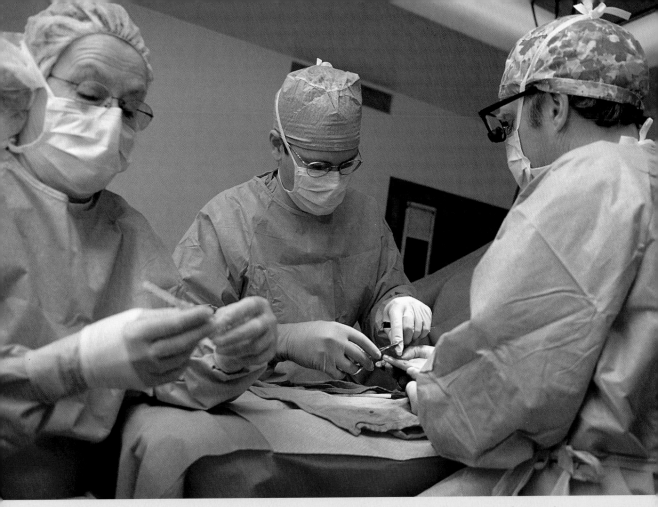

Here, a patient gets hand surgery, which is very delicate and requires a team of doctors.

Most of the time, when Dr. Campbell is called to the Emergency Room, it is to fix a broken bone. Fractured, or broken bones can happen while playing sports, or during an accident such as a fall.

Dr. Campbell might also be needed in the Emergency Room if a patient has a deep cut that has damaged a tendon or nerve. This is one of the reasons why orthopedists are trained surgeons.

HOW DOES A BONE HEAL?

Bones are very hard and strong. They are made of a combination of many things, including a lot of calcium. It is hard to imagine that once they break, bones can heal together again. But they can. How does your body do this?

When a bone breaks, blood thickens (clots) around the broken ends of the bone. Then, special cells called *osteoblasts* (bone-forming cells) travel to the spaces that were made by the break. These cells form fibers made of protein. The fibers grow between the broken edges of bone.

When this happens, new bone is actually growing! The material that grows is called *callus*. The callus slowly hardens to become calcium, which becomes new bone. This new bone eventually becomes as strong as the original bone!

This whole amazing process only takes about 8 to 10 weeks in children. It takes a few weeks longer for adult bones to heal.

1
A blood clot forms between bone ends.

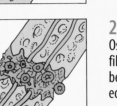

2
Osteoblasts form fibers that grow between the broken edges of the bone.

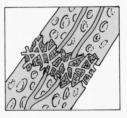

3
New bone (callus) is laid down between the bone ends and over the fracture line.

4
Remodeling takes place, with more dense, stronger bone laid down.

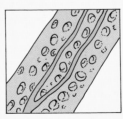

5
Over a period of weeks, the bone returns to its original shape.

When he is not at the hospital, Dr. Campbell is seeing patients in his office.

The first thing Dr. Campbell does is ask his patients what brings them to his office. Is it something they've noticed for a long time? Did they fall off their bike? Then Dr. Campbell gives them a physical exam. As part of the exam, he gently moves a patient's joints around to see if anything causes pain.

After an exam, Dr. Campbell might give a patient three different kinds of tests. He might have an X-ray taken. He might do a muscle strength test. Or he might do a nerve test. Sometimes he does all three! None of these tests hurt.

Several people in the office help an orthopedist. For example, a nurse or a technician will take an X-ray. An X-ray is actually a picture of your skeleton! It gives an orthopedist a clear view of the broken bone. Once Dr. Campbell sees it, he knows exactly how to fix it.

A patient must stand very still for an X-ray.

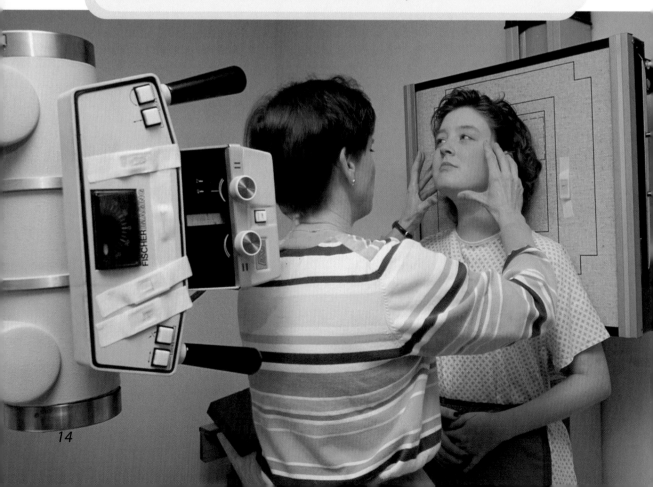

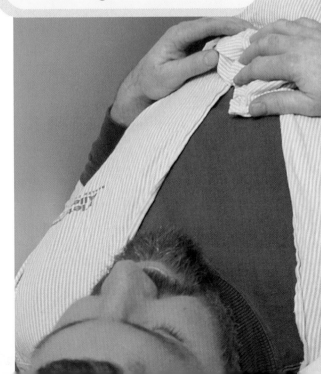

A muscle strength test will show Dr. Campbell if any nerves have been injured. It will also tell him if a patient has any pain. This test is usually done by asking the patient to push or pull against pressure applied by the doctor's hands.

If Dr. Campbell thinks a nerve may be damaged, he will do some nerve testing. He may try different ways of testing reflexes. Or he may check for feeling in the skin.

Dr. Campbell does a muscle strength test.
Inset: *Testing a patient's reflexes*

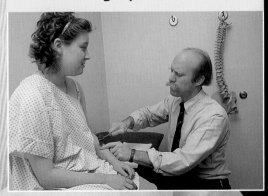

If a bone is broken, it must be treated and then wrapped in some way. In order to heal properly, the area where a bone has broken cannot move. Before doing this, Dr. Campbell looks carefully at what the X-ray tells him.

Dr. Campbell reviews a hand X-ray with a young patient.

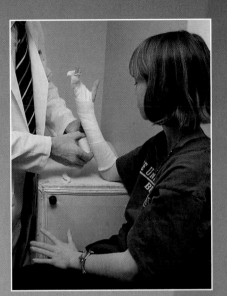

Once in a while, a bone break is crooked and needs to be lined up. To do this, Dr. Campbell lightly pushes on the bone to straighten it.

Then a cast is put on. It goes on in three layers. First a netting is put on the arm. Then it is wrapped with a padding (see inset photo).

17

Finally, it is covered with fiberglass. The fiberglass comes in rolls of many different colors (see inset photo). Dr. Campbell dips the fiberglass cast material in water. Then he wraps it around the area with the broken bone.

Once he is finished, Dr. Campbell holds the cast in place for a few minutes while it dries quickly. Within ten minutes, the completely dry cast is as hard as a rock!

In several weeks, the bone will heal. At that point, Dr. Campbell will cut the cast off. Don't worry, this never hurts—but the machine he uses is very noisy!

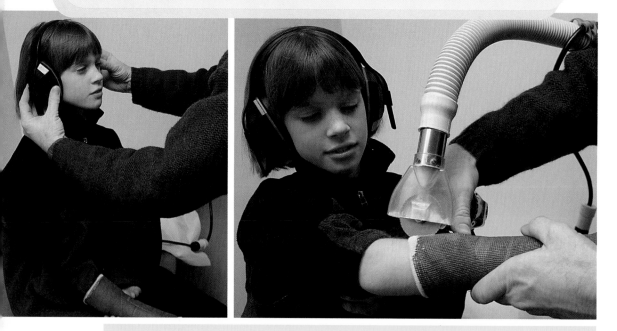

Above left: *Ear pads block out the noise as a cast is cut.*
Above right: *The cast is cut with a tiny saw.*
Below: *Scissors are used for the final removal of the cast.*

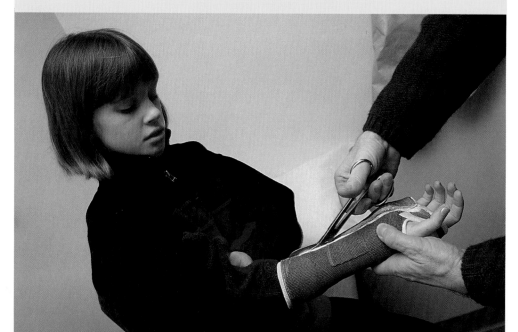

A big part of an orthopedist's day is spent answering the many questions that patients have. Some of this takes place during an office visit. But lots of patients think of questions or have worries when they are not in the office. Because doctors are so busy during the day, patients often have to leave messages. Toward the end of the day, Dr. Campbell spends a lot of time on the phone. That's when he returns all his messages.

Dr. Campbell takes a few moments at the end of the day to relax with one of the instruments he plays.

Dr. Campbell says he became an orthopedist because "it makes me happy to help people". When he thinks about all the people he helps, he is proud to be a doctor. And when he cuts a cast off a patient and sees a bone that has healed as good as new, he knows he has been a part of something very special.

Glossary

fracture (frakt•chur) A crack, split, or break—as in a bone.

ligaments (lig•a•mentz) A band of strong tissue that connects two bones together.

osteoblast (oss•tee•o•blast) A cell that develops into bone.

pediatrician (pee•dee•a•tri•shun) A doctor that specializes in the care of children.

radiologist (ray•dee•ol•o•gist) A doctor that specializes in the science that deals with X-rays and other forms of radiant energy to diagnose and treat disease.

tendons (ten•dunz) A band of strong tissue that attaches a muscle to a bone or other part of the body.

vertebrate (ver•te•brayt) Any of a large group of animals having a backbone, a skeleton of bone or cartilage, and a brain enclosed in a skull.

Further Reading

Balestrino, Philip. *The Skeleton Inside You.* New York: HarperCollins, 1989.

Bauer, Judith. *What's It Like to Be a Doctor?* New York: Troll, 1990.

Drescher, Joan. *Your Doctor, My Doctor.* New York: Walker & Co., 1987.

Ganeri, Anita. *Moving.* Mahwah, NJ: Raintree-Steck Vaughn, 1994.

Woods, Samuel. *The Pediatrician* (Doctors In Action series). Woodbridge, CT: Blackbirch Press, 1999.

Index